The Pocket Guide to
Hold 'Em Poker

The Pocket Guide to
Hold 'Em Poker

Ted Pannell

BURFORD BOOKS

Printed in the United States of America.

10   9   8   7   6   5   4   3   2   1

Library of Congress Cataloging-in-Publication Data
is on file with the Library of Congress.

ISBN: 1-58080-141-2
ISBN-13: 978-1-58080-141-6

*To my wife, Sylvia, who has
filled the inside straight in my life
with love and happiness.*

Contents

Introduction

This guide is for the new player who wants to have the edge in the most exciting game ever to hit the green felt . . . Texas Hold 'Em Poker.

If you're already a Hold 'Em player and wondering what you're doing wrong, this guide will help your game. Using these tips, your play will become almost automatic with the first two cards. You'll be more composed and self-assured at the table, knowing you're playing the best cards possible. This alone will enhance your game psychologically. You'll know when to hold 'em, fold 'em, be slow, or be bold.

Don't worry: I won't burden you with charts, figures, odds, and percentages to remember. Rather, I'll give you a solid foundation for playing a steadfast game. These tips and guidelines can be applied to private games or to casino play. If you're a new player, read this and other Hold 'Em books, and practice, practice, practice. A home game should have comfortable limits for you. When you're starting in the casino, I recommend sitting in the game with the lowest limit—generally $2/4 and $3/6.

Back in the 1970s, there was little interest in Hold 'Em; few Nevada casinos even offered the game. The World Series of Poker and the Super Bowl of Poker were the only major tournaments at the time. Now there are hundreds being held everywhere. I've been playing and writing about poker for years and, while living near Lake Tahoe and Reno, watched it transform into the most popular poker game in world. Most said it was too complicated. You're about to find out how simple it really is.

These days Hold 'Em is played all over the world as well as on TV, exotic islands, cruise ships, and riverboat casinos; in Europe, Nevada, New Jersey, and Native American casinos across the United States; even on the computer. Yes, on your computer. You can practice free by playing thousands of hands on poker Web sites. You can also enter free online tournaments with a chance at winning millions. Or the prize could be a buy-in to a major tournament, most often held on television or in fabulous Las Vegas. Monetary games can be played on the Internet using your credit card. But whoa, remember it's real money.

There are tourneys for amateurs, semipros, professionals, celebrities, movie stars, and athletes. All you need is the buy-in. You can also get into prime tournaments for free by winning satellite games, which are held leading up to the main event. This is a tough road to travel, however, because you're competing against thousands of players for just one spot.

The World Series of Poker (WSOP) determines the World Poker Champion with a Hold 'Em game. It's played once a year in Las Vegas, Nevada, and broadcast on TV. The buy-in is $10,000, and anyone can enter. The no-limit play continues until one player is left. Over the years, the number of players has increased to thousands, with a grand prize of a gold-and-diamond bracelet and millions of dollars. The 2006—37th annual—WSOP drew a record field of 8,773 entrants. The last remaining 12 players were guaranteed at least $1.5 million in winnings. The winner won an astonishing grand prize of $12 million. Sound exciting? You bet.

Rank of Hands

Here is the order in which Hold 'Em hands rank, from highest to lowest, without a wild card. In casino poker rooms, wild cards are not used, but that's not to say you can't use them in a home or private game.

royal flush	A–K–Q–J–10 same suit
straight flush	any five consecutive cards, 2-through–K, same suit
four of a kind	A–A–A–A–x
full house	A–A–A–K–K (any three of a kind, along with any pair)
flush	all the same suit (Hearts, Clubs, et cetera)
straight	any five consecutive cards, 2-through–A, unsuited
three of a kind	A–A–A–x–x
two pair	A–A–K–K–x
one pair	A–A–x–x–x

Hold 'Em Terms

There are more terms and slang words related to poker and particularly Hold 'Em than almost any other game. Gamblers have always been notorious for slapping nicknames onto games of chance, of course—even onto the players themselves. Just watch a tournament on TV and you'll see what I mean.

You'll find that the following terms are all vital for your knowledge of the game and its rules. Study them carefully, for it's important to know your way around the language.

all in: To bet all the chips or money you have left on the table. A player will announce, "I'm all in." Some players will push their chips toward the center of the table to indicate that they're betting everything—they've put themselves all in.

ante: The amount of money or chips that each player puts up to begin each round of play. In a home game, each player might put in 25 cents or more. In the casino, the ante is called a *blind*. The amount varies.

bad beat: A bad loss, especially an unusual one. For example, having a strong hand beaten by a stronger hand—such as seeing your four of a kind lose after an opponent draws the one card needed to fill a straight flush—is a bad beat.

blind: The same as the *ante*. The amount put up by the two players left of the *button*, meaning that they're making a blind bet before the hand is dealt. Generally, there are two blinds, a small blind, and a big blind. Using chips as an example, a small blind would be two chips; a big blind, four chips. The blinds move to the left after each game so every player will be on the blinds during a session. The amount of the blind is determined by the game limit.

bluff: To mislead by a pretense of strength. That is, to bet or raise with a lousy hand.

board: The five *community cards* turned faceup on the table, starting with the *flop*. If, for example, the flop is 8-J-5, a *4th Street* is K; a *5th Street*, 2.

bullets: Slang for Aces.

burn card: The dealer always burns, or buries the top card from the deck before dealing each hand. In Hold 'Em, there is a burn card between each round of the hand, beginning before the first two *pocket* cards are dealt. A card is burned before the *flop*, and before *4th Street* and *5th Street*. This dates back to times when players regularly cheated. The taking of the first card breaks up any card stacking, just as would cutting the deck before playing a hand.

button: Since casino poker has a fixed dealer, an object or disk with the word DEALER on it is placed in front of a player to indicate the potential dealer; he or she is "on the button." After each game, it's passed to the left, giving everyone an opportunity to be the "dealer." This position is the last to act.

buy-in: The amount of money it takes to sit in a game. In a private game, the buy-in is usually whatever amount you intend to play with, or no less than what the host has set. In a casino, the buy-in varies according to the limits of the game. Casino games are table stakes—that is, only the amount of chips you have on the table can be played; there's no adding of chips or cash in the middle of a hand. Find a limit you're comfortable with and that fits within your budget.

call: To equal the amount of chips a player has bet or raised; players will say, "I call" that amount.

check: If you don't want to bet your hand, you can check it. However, if a bet has already been made, you cannot check; you have to *call* an equal amount.

check-raise: To check your hand then raise after another player has bet. When you're holding or catching strong cards, rather than bet it—as you normally would—you can choose to check it. If a player bets, you'd then come back with a raise. So you would first check your good hand, then raise it. This is a maneuver designed to get more chips into the pot, and it works best on *5th Street*.

community cards: The cards that are turned faceup on the table. All the players use this stack to make hands by combining them with one or both of their *pocket* or hole cards. The five combined cards are also known as the *board*.

connectors: Cards that are coupled or linked together in a series—for example, 7-8 or 4-5—are known as connected or connector cards.

dump: To fold your hand—also called a laydown or muck—is to dump the hand.

5th Street: The fifth up card on the *board*, also known as the River Card.

flop: The first three cards turned faceup consecutively by the dealer.

4th Street: The fourth up card after the *flop* on the *board*, also called the Turn Card.

hand: The five cards that make up a round of poker can be called "a hand of poker."

heads-up: Two players going against each other, also known as one-on-one.

high end: The high card of a straight, a straight flush, or a hand. If you have 7-8-9-10-J, you're on the high end with the Jack.

ignorant end: The low end of a straight. If the flop comes 8-9-10, you should be holding J-Q, not 6-7. Drawing to the low side is called "drawing to the ignorant end."

inside draw or inside straight: Needing a card in the middle, or inside, of a *connector* to complete a straight. If you have 7-8-10-J, for instance, you need a 9 to make your straight, which is drawing to the inside.

kicker: The next highest unpaired card that determines the winner of two poker hands of equal value: a tiebreaker. Two 9s with a King beats two 9s with a Queen.

kill game: When a player wins two hands in a row, the game limit doubles—a $3/6 game, for example, doubles to $6/12. The game continues until that same player loses, and the game reverts to its original limits.

lay down: To fold or quit your hand is to lay down.

limp in: To be reluctant or slow in calling a bet or coming into a hand. This can occur when players are holding questionable cards. Limping in can also be an act, as in *sandbagging* or slow playing a strong hand.

loose player: Someone whose play is erratic, and/or who plays most hands with almost any combination of cards. He or she generally has more luck than skill and is usually a losing player.

nuts: Cards that give you the absolute winner, or prevent another player from making a higher hand. Let's say you have A-5 Clubs, and three Clubs are on the board. No player can hold the Ace Club to beat your flush in this case—because you have it, the nut flush.

Omaha Hold 'Em: A variation not to be confused with Texas Hold 'Em. In Omaha, you are dealt four *pocket* cards, of which two must be used in combination with three cards from the *board* to make up your five-card hand.

on the come: A player with a good hand looking to improve is said to be on the come—say, one who has a four straight or four flush and is looking to complete it with the fifth card.

open end: This refers to a four-straight or straight-flush draw that needs a card (*connector*) on either end to complete the hand.

paints: Face cards—Jacks, Queens, and Kings. Jacks are also called Hooks, Queens are Ladies, and Kings are Cowboys.

pocket: The first two down cards you are dealt are in your pocket, also called hole cards.

position: A player's betting position in relation to the *button* and *blinds*. The front or early position (bets first) is behind the blinds. The last or late position (bets last) is the button.

preflop: Action taking place before the *flop*. Your first two cards would be preflop cards.

rags: This term generally refers to low, unsuited, unplayable cards; 2-6-9 would be considered a rag *flop*, for example, while a 3-8 unsuited in the *pocket* would be a rag hand.

rainbow flop: A *flop* of three cards of different suits, which prevents a flush from being made on *4th Street*. All five *community cards* can be a rainbow *board*—no flush can be made, having only two of the same suit.

read: To analyze what a player's cards might be is to read them. You can also read (analyze) a player, mannerisms, or style of play to determine if he or she is bluffing or holding a strong or weak hand.

river: The last card dealt up on the board, referred to as "Down the River" or just the "River Card."

sandbagging: Playing a big hand as if it's weak to keep other players in the pot. Instead of betting, you will be checking or calling then betting heavy on the end. This is related to the *slow play*.

semibluff: Betting a small hand, such as a low pair or even a high card, as if it were strong. This isn't completely a bluff, because the hand could still win against a weaker one.

slow play: Playing a strong pair or a good combination as if it were weak. That is, checking or making a minimal bet on a good hand, hoping to pull in players. It's similar to *sandbagging*.

short stack: If your stack of chips is low or you're losing, you're playing with a short stack.

suited cards: Cards are suited if they are of the same suit, such as all Hearts or all Spades.

tells: Nervous little habits a player might display when on a good hand or bluffing, such as tapping fingers or quick puffs on a cigarette. A player may also become very quiet.

tight: This term refers to a player who plays few hands, and mostly with cards that stand to win.

trips: Three of a kind.

turn card: The *4th Street* up card on the *board*.

unsuited cards: Cards are unsuited if they are of mixed suits, such as 2 Clubs, 4 Hearts, 6 Diamonds.

wheel: The lowest possible straight you can get: A-2-3-4-5.

wired: Being dealt a pair. To have any pair in the *pocket*.

How It's Played

As Hold 'Em gained popularity, some folks began to compare it to Seven Card Stud, but many hard-core Hold 'Em players say "No way." As in Seven Stud, seven cards are used, but this is where the similarity ends. In Hold 'Em, five of the seven cards used by all the players are exposed. You only have to determine what two cards a player might have started with in the hole.

Play begins after the players have put up their antes; in a casino, these are called blinds. The dealer will burn a card (discard it facedown, not to be used in the game); then each player is dealt two cards facedown. The player to the left of the blinds is the first to act and remains first throughout that hand. A bet is made on these two cards at this time. After the betting is finished, the dealer will burn another card then deal the flop—three cards faceup on the table in front of him or her. These are called community cards, and all the players combine them with their two existing hole cards or pocket cards to make their hand. After a round of betting, another card is burned and a fourth card is turned up. This card is called

4th Street or the Turn Card. The remaining players will bet again.

Last, another card is burned and then a fifth card is turned up, called 5th Street or the River Card. All the cards dealt faceup are known collectively as the board. There is a final round of betting on 5th Street. The player with the best five of the seven cards is the winner.

It's possible to have a split pot if the remaining players will have equal hands by using the cards on the board. Let's say that after 5th Street, a Spade flush is on the board. If no player holds a higher Spade in his or her hand, the remaining players can use the cards on the board, giving them a flush—the pot would be split.

This situation (split pot) is also possible with straights. If you have K-Q in the pocket, your opponent has A-K, and the board shows J-Q-10-A-4, both hands are an Ace high straight. Thus you both win, splitting the pot.

Note: If your opponent is betting with you after the flop, the reason could be that he or she is betting on three Jacks, Queens, or 10s and is on the come for a full house.

With experience, you will come to recognize playable pocket cards and know when to bet, raise, call, or lay down. The flop will determine the value of your hand and whether you should stay or fold. Continuing through 4th and 5th Streets will show how your starting hand develops into a winner or loser.

Luck plays a more important role in Hold 'Em than many players like to believe. Skill comes in the betting and knowledge of your pocket cards. After the initial round of betting, you are at the mercy of the community cards, and they will dictate how you bet. No matter how good a player you think you are, no amount of skill can overcome poor cards turning up on the board to break your hand.

Sample Poker Hand

You have pocket Aces; your opponent has K-Q. The flop comes: A-A-K. You have four Aces; your opponent has two pair, Kings and Aces. Fourth Street is another King. You still have four Aces but now your opponent has a full house, Kings over Aces. The River Card or 5th Street is a 7, no good to either of you.

As you can see from the Rank of Hands, below, your four Aces have beaten the full house. Your opponent's full house probably led him or her to believe a win was assured, and he or she likely bet heavily.

THE FLOP

4th Street   5th Street

you have
4 ACES

opponent
FULL HOUSE,
KINGS
OVER ACES

Sample Split Pot

You're dealt J-Q; your opponent, J-10. The flop comes 8-9-10. You have a Queen high straight. Your opponent has a pair of 10s and a possible straight draw, open on both ends for a 7 or Queen. Fourth Street turns up a Queen. Now your opponent has a Queen high straight, the same as you. The 5th Street comes in with a 4, which is no help to either of you.

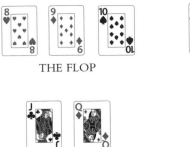

THE FLOP

4th   5th
Street   Street

you hold   opponent

Both hands have a Queen High Straight

Best Starting Hands Guide

With experience, you'll be able to weight any two-card combinations against others. Obviously, the higher your cards, the greater the advantage you enjoy.

In a private low-limit game, you can play a little loose and start with almost any combination, then determine if you have a playable hand after the flop. In the casino, follow the starting hands more closely and play tighter.

Here are the best two-card combinations for starting hands, giving you the edge over your opponents. As in any poker game, Aces are the big guns.

Best Starting Hands

A-A (this is the very best hand)

10-through-K paired

10-through-A suited

10-through-A unsuited, connected

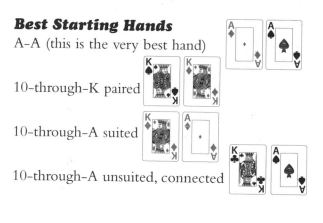

Decent Hands

2-through-9 paired

5-through-9 suited for straight-flush draw—say,
5-6 Hearts, 7-8 Clubs, 8-9 Spades

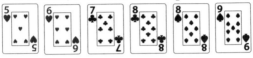

A-through-9 unsuited, connected for straight
draw—say, A-2, A-3, A-4, A-5, 6-7, 7-8, 8-9

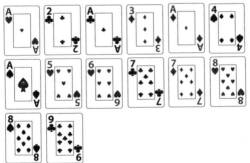

Trouble Hands

Small unsuited cards, such as
3 Diamonds, 7 Spades;
or 4 Hearts, 8 Clubs

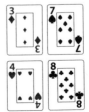

High-low unsuited cards, such as K Hearts, 4 Clubs; or J Diamonds, 2 Spades

Ace-middle unsuited, unconnected cards, such as A-6 or A-8

Summary

For your starting cards before the flop, look to play:

- High pairs
- High suited cards
- High straight cards

Your First Two Cards Before the Flop

One of the most often asked questions about Hold 'Em is: How do I play my first two cards? The answer is simple: Tough. This is where you become a bulldog. When you're meeting a person for the first time, you want to make a lasting impression. So it is with your first two cards—you want to impress your competitors.

Your chance of winning more pots improves when you have the advantage of starting with the best possible cards. Thus, you must bet them. You don't have a complete hand yet and need to remove some competition. At this point, you aren't concerned with keeping players in; what you want is having few as possible to deal with—best of all, getting into a one-on-one situation.

Keep in mind that you're better off having one player call a five-chip bet than five players calling a one-chip bet. The amount is the same, but in the latter case you'll have five players trying to outdraw you, and odds are that one or more of them may do just that. So thin out the field as quickly as possible. No matter what you have after the flop, the remaining players will have to respect your first action.

You'll have a strong indication of what cards to play or back off with after studying the Best Starting Hands Guide, above. Beginning with the Ace combinations, let's go through the best starting cards and look at how they might be played.

Playing the Ace

Generally, Ace with a low card is a troubled combo and should see limited action. It can be a great hand . . . or just a pain in the Ace.

I suggest that it's okay to play the Ace with a smaller unsuited card before the flop within limited conditions. A combination such as A-3 should be played like a small pair. If you don't improve on the flop, get rid of it. What you're really looking for in playing this type of hand is Aces or better.

Play the Ace with small unsuited card for a straight draw: A-2, -3, -4, or -5.

Let's say you start with A-5 unsuited in the pocket, your opponent has A-10, and the flop brings A-9-3. Your straight did not happen, but you both have Aces and your opponent is ahead with his 10 high kicker. As you can see, playing an Ace with a low card can be dangerous.

When playing the A-K or A-10 for a straight draw, be aware that if you should hit a four straight on the flop, it will be open only on one end or to the inside. There are two more cards coming—a gamble worth taking, perhaps.

Play the Ace suited with middle card for a flush draw: A-7 Hearts or A-9 Hearts. If you don't improve after the flop to Aces paired, straight, or flush—or at least a four straight or four flush draw—consider folding in the course of heavy betting.

High-Low Combinations

As a rule, high and low unsuited cards—such as K-2, Q-3, or 10-5—should not be played together. You have neither the straight nor the flush working for you.

The only exception might be, as I have said before, if you can get into a pot for little or nothing, looking to catch a better hand. If you feel like bucking the odds to change your luck or style of play, it could be worth the gamble. Should you make it through to a high-card showdown, the next highest card determines the winner, and your low card now becomes suspect. This type of pairing will only get you in trouble—novice players fall in love with high cards. Don't be one of them. Abort this type of hand and wait for a better one.

Playing Straights

You have a better hand if you play connecting cards such as 5-6, 8-9, J-Q, or Q-K. The A-K is open on one end only; the A-10 is open inside only. It's extremely hard trying to play high-low combination for straights, such as 9–K or 6-10. This is a stretch for the inside draw, and odds are not in your favor. Again, if you can see the flop for nothing or a minimal bet, you might consider staying. Overall, though, prospects aren't good. If you miss a four straight on the flop, get out. If you pair, you then have to reassess the probability of continuing. Remember, it's so much cleaner to just play connecting cards, high or low.

Playing Flushes

Suited combinations with a high card, such as A-6 or K-3, are much better, and the flop comes with lower cards to your suit. Holding the Ace or other high cards gives you a chance at the high-end flush. If you only catch a three-card flush on the flop, consider folding. Ideally, you need to hit a four flush to consider staying in the hand. Playing low suits is subject to failure, because it only takes a single higher-card flush to beat you. You'll see many flushes made in this game.

After the Flop

So what happens in Texas Hold 'Em after the flop? Let me give you some suggestions on how you can play the various hands you might be presented with.

Whatever pocket cards you receive, the flop determines if you have a possible winning hand. Though you might improve, the strength of your hand still depends on what cards you hold and what cards are on the board. Don't forget that 4th and 5th Street are still to come.

What makes this game so popular are the many ways to make a hand due to the community cards on the board. You can expect to be looking down the barrel at possible straights, flushes, and full houses, even four of a kinds and straight flushes, though seldom the royal flush.

At times, a small pair can win as well as a high card. Under certain conditions, you can win this way if you're daring enough to play to the end. It doesn't always take a great hand to win the pot. Any win is a good win—not to mention the thrill it adds to the game.

The Pair

Under normal conditions, almost any pair is a betting or calling hand on the preflop. Large pairs, such as 10s through Aces, are truly the better cards before the flop. If the pair increases to trips or two pair, you have a shot at a full house with 4th and 5th Street coming.

If you don't improve, you still could hold high pair. Should everyone check, you can bet it up to drop players. You will have to assess your hand along with the investment. What is it going to cost to see more cards?

With a small pair, you may find yourself in an uneasy position. The small pair alone won't win many pots. You can play it very tough on the first two cards, but if they don't develop into three of a kind or two pair on the flop, they probably should be dumped in the midst of heavy betting. The exception would be if you could limp into 4th Street and 5th Street. Then, should you catch trips or two pair, you're back in the game.

The small pair can also be a good candidate for the semibluff, given the right circumstances. That is, before the flop, bet or raise the bettor.

This tactic may cause your opponents to lay down or check on the flop. Whether you stay or fold after the flop depends on the strength of the pair and the wagering. Most players love the big pair, but when small pair improve, they can be very rewarding. Don't overlook their possibilities.

Two Pair

Are the two pair open or concealed? There are two situations to weigh here. First, you can have one pair in the pocket—say, J-J, and the flop shows 7-7-10 (open). At this point, you not only have one hidden pair, but you have the high end with J-7s. Be aware that, with a pair on the board, someone might have trips (three of a kind), or also have two pair. If you're first to act, you can bet or check and see what action you get. Betting and raising sends up a red flag; play with caution. If you don't make a full house by 5th Street, you'll have to decide if your two pair is strong enough to take the pot.

The second situation is much better. Your pocket cards are (for instance) J-7, and the flop comes J-7-8. Now both your pair are con-cealed, and the chances of an opponent having trips in this flop are smaller. You still hold the high pair of Jacks with 7s. If you're first to act, be aggressive. If not, raise when it's your turn. You still have 4th and 5th Streets coming; don't make it easy on the remaining players.

Three of a Kind

Just as with two pair: Are your trips concealed—a pair in the pocket and one on the board? Take, for example, a 7-7 in the pocket and 7-9-Q on the board. In this case, no problem. You can do a lot of betting without giving up much information. Should a Queen or 9 land on 4th or 5th Street, be conscious of someone having higher trips.

If your trips are open, however—say, 7-7 on the board and one 7 in the pocket—your prospects aren't as good. A pair on the board may mean an opponent having three of a kind or two pair. Just as important, do you have a high kicker with your trips? With 7-7 on the board, do you hold a high card in the pocket such as 7-K? Here, you want to bet with 4th and 5th Street still to come. You could make a full house—but so could your opponent. You can usually play this hand to 5th Street.

Straights and Flushes

If you start with a two-card straight or flush and catch a third card on the flop, you can call or make a minimal bet; it's not wise to bet any more at this point. Your odds of catching two cards in a row aren't good. If you can stay for nothing, do so; if not, it's time to blow. The important question with straights and flushes is, Do you hold the nuts—Ace high straight or Ace high flush?

Should you catch four cards with the flop, you can bet if you're first to act or raise when it's your turn. Don't worry about dropping players with a raise. You want few callers here. Two cards are still to come; your odds are a little better, since you only need one.

With a four straight on the flop, it's better to have it open on both ends. With a four flush, you want your pocket cards higher than what's on the board. You can usually play these hands to 5th Street.

If you get a straight or flush on the flop, you must bet it. With a three-card straight or flush on the board, chances are that at least one player will be on the come with the same hand. Unless you hold the nuts, pay attention if a player calls or raises.

Full House

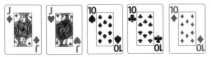

Catching a full house on the flop is extraordinarily unlikely, to say the least. A full house can come in two ways. The best way to explain this is illustrate it.

First, you can have (say) J-J in the pocket, and 10-10-10 on the board. With this board, it's likely someone could have four of a kind or another full house plus having a pair in the pocket. Remember, you don't always have to bet; you can call in the face of heavy betting. In this position, play with caution, realizing that your full house can be beat. If possible, play to the end. This is still a good hand, and you don't want to just give the pot away.

The second possibility, of course, is the best scenario, with J-10 in the pocket and J-10-10 on the board; now the chances of someone having four of a kind are nil. Your competition is likely to hold three of a kind or two pair.

You can sandbag this hand or even bet if you feel it won't scare off players. You have a very strong hand.

In low-limit poker—which is what you should be playing—you can't get hurt badly by calling if you're unsure, or raising if you strongly feel you have the best hand.

Four of a Kind

Catching four of a kind on the flop gives you fewer options and fewer things to consider than other high hands. For example, you can have J-J in the pocket and J-J-Q on the board. This can give your opponent two pair or a full house should he have Q-Q in the pocket. Remember, you can be beat if an opponent holds a higher pair in the pocket, and two of the same cards drop on 4th or 5th Street . . . although the odds of that happening are low. That would be a very, very bad beat.

You can slow play to keep players in or make modest bets. You want to give the "on the come" players a chance to make their full house, trips, or whatever. So try to milk this situation to build the pot as much as possible. If there's betting, raising, and reraising going on, just call. If you play too hard too soon, you'll lose players and not get the payoff you'd otherwise expect. The downside of letting players stay in, however, is that someone may draw out on you.

At the end, unload on the remaining players, check-raise, raise, or whatever is possible. If your opponent thinks you have trips or a lower full house, you'll get return action. Then you can lower the boom.

The Straight Flush

If you're lucky enough to get a straight flush in the first five cards, determine if you hold the nuts—the card or cards that prevent a higher straight flush. If not, proceed with care. There will be three cards to a straight flush on the board, which puts other promising hands out there. By the River Card (5th Street), there could be a lower or higher straight flush.

Examine the cards and players closely. You don't want to start your end-zone dance too early.

If you have the nuts, though, no problem. Slow play it.

The Royal Flush

Wow! A poker player's dream. If you make "The Royal," you should . . . jump up on your chair, do a little dance, pump your fist, and yell *"Yes."* Just kidding! That might give your hand away . . . you think?

For once in your poker life, you have an unbeatable hand. Milk it, sandbag it, slow play it—whatever it takes to keep players in. Pray that someone sitting there has a betting hand. Even if opponents suspect (after you sit down) that you might have the big R, they'll probably call at the end just to see it. So good luck!

How to Practice

It's very important to prepare yourself before a game. I strongly encourage you to practice in your spare time and just before you play. Consider it a warm-up—the kind you'd do in any professional sport. Athletes will run, jump, throw, and catch before competing—whatever they need to ready themselves for the action ahead. It shouldn't be any different for a poker player. Prepare yourself mentally and physically.

You can get poker Web site addresses from TV poker programs and go online to play. There you can play thousands of hands free—this, too, will give you some advantage. Still, only practice with real cards will give you a feel for hands-on play. Deal several hands as shown in Practice Hands.

Playing out dummy hands will get you familiar with the good starting cards and help you recognize a playable hand instantly. These practice sessions give you both confidence and the satisfaction of knowing that you're making the correct plays. For a home or private game, deal out the number of hands, generally five to six players. When you feel you're ready to play in the casino, practice by dealing out no less than nine or ten.

Burn and deal out the number of hands just as you would in a game, only faceup. After you have two cards for each player, pause and study each of them. Using the Best Starting Hands Guide, determine which are your best, decent, and troubled hands. After you eliminate what you consider poor or weak cards, push them aside—but don't turn them over. You'll want to see how they stand at the end.

Next, burn a card and turn the flop. Study the cards again, betting, folding, raising, and reraising as if each hand were your own. Burn another card and turn 4th Street; is there any change for the better? Are there any hands to discard? Deal 5th Street, following the same procedure.

Now that you have a winner, check the hands you discarded earlier and determine if they had a chance. You will recognize that almost any combination can win at some point, including small cards and mixed high-low hands.

Overall, though, you'll find that the high-card alliances and pairs will win more pots than those you discarded. Odd groupings are seldom worth playing.

Let's look at some sample practice hands.

Practice Hands

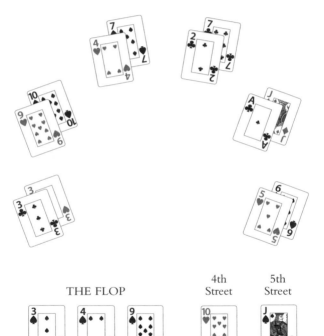

| | THE FLOP | | 4th Street | 5th Street |

Practice Hands Explanation

You have dealt six sets of hands, and 1st Player is first to act.

1st Player: Pair of 3s. Decent starting hand; see the flop.

2nd Player: 9 Hearts and 10 Spades. Possible straight; see the flop.

3rd Player: 4 Hearts, 7 Spades. No good; fold. These cards are too small, and drawing to the inside is never a good play.

4th Player: 2-7 Clubs. A possible flush; see the flop.

5th Player: Ace Clubs, J Diamonds. Ace high and possible straight draw; see the flop.

6th Player: 5 Hearts, 6 Spades. A possible low straight. This is a weak hand; stay for the flop if the price is right.

First Player has a decent starting hand; he can draw to trips or two pair. He really needs to hit trips on the flop—he bets. Second Player has a straight draw open on both ends and can still get high carded. She can call or raise—it's better to raise. Fourth Player has a risky low flush draw. Should he catch his flush, it can be beat by a higher flush. He calls. Fifth Player has the best

starting cards with possibilities of a straight or
Aces on the flop. Also, it's a raising hand before
the flop—she can call or raise. Sixth Player has
a low straight draw, open on both ends. Like the
low flush, it's not that great. A lot depends on
the flop and the betting—he just calls.

Flop: 3-4-9 Spades

1st Player: Has three 3s (trips). Stays.

2nd Player: Pair of 9s and possible 10 high flush.
    Stays.

4th Player: No flush. Folds.

5th Player: Nothing possible. Folds.

6th Player: Possible straight, possible flush. Stays.

First Player will bet. Second Player will call,
or maybe raise. Sixth Player's straight and flush
are small; he should probably fold in lieu of
heavy betting. With three small Spades on the
board, it's likely that someone holds larger
Spades. Still, there are options, and each person
will play it differently. First, 6th Player can call
to try to catch a straight or flush. Second, he can
reraise to try to drop one of his opponents. For
the sake of example, let's say he calls or reraises
and stays in.

4th Street: 10 Hearts

1st Player: Stills has three 3s.

2nd Player: Now has two pair 9s and 10s and possible 10 high flush.

6th Player: No improvement.

First Player can still bet or just check. Second Player can call a bet or reraise; with only one card coming, she has a possible flush or full–house draw. Sixth Player just calls here. He can still make a straight or flush on 5th Street. How much does he want to invest on one more card, and could he win if he gets his hand? Let's keep him in.

5th Street: J Spade

1st Player: Still three 3s.

2nd Player: Has made a J high flush.

6th Player: Has also made a J high flush.

The Showdown

1st Player's trips were good but not good enough.

2nd Player wins with her J-10 flush.

6th Player loses with his J-9 flush. His starting hand was a little low to begin with, and in view of the heavy betting, he probably should have folded earlier.

Now You Try It

| | THE FLOP | | 4th Street | 5th Street |

Note: For the results of these practice hands, see page 75.

Helpful Tips

- **If you don't have something at the beginning, don't stay to the end.** I put this tip first because it's perhaps the most valuable, sensible, and reasonable strategy of them all. It will save you a lot of money and heartache. It'll also keep you from getting yourself in a bad position. When you see your first two cards, ask yourself if they're worth staying for. If you have to think too long about it, you should probably fold. In low-limit, loose home games, you can usually see more flops. At higher limits, though, keep to this rule.

- **For the most part, play tight.** Play fewer hands and only with cards that give you a chance to win the pot. Be aggressive—an aggressive player is typically a winning player. Watch for tight players. They're usually on good hands when they're in the action. A tight player is easier to bluff than a loose one.

- **Put all your money on the table** in a private game. Having to dig when you want to bet a strong hand will give it away. In casino games, however, no digging. You can buy extra chips between hands; just ask the dealer.

- **Play the same when you're sure of your cards as when you're not.** If you habitually look at your cards when you're uncertain, do the same when you're on a good hand. If you have a pair of strong cards in the pocket, they're easy to remember. You don't have to keep double-checking. Watch for this behavior in your opponents.

- **Play the same when you're winning as when you're losing.** Don't let the amount of money on the table alter your style. If you have an excellent hand and only a few chips, or a short stack, go all in. You have nothing to lose. If you have plenty of chips, bet the limit or slow play. It's usually wisest to play your strong hands as aggressively as possible, regardless of how many chips you have.

- **Become a vigil player** when you're not in a hand. Watch and listen for tells, such as an opponent saying, "A little help, dealer." Such pleading could mean he or she is on the come. Inexperienced players are seldom conscious of verbal tells; they remain unaware that what they say is important to the serious player. Any little thing can be useful information to a spy—be a 007 at the table.

- **Don't throw out your weak hands until it's your turn.** If everyone throws out, you'll win—*if* you're still in. If everyone checks, consider a bluff. If the bet is checked to you, you can check and see a free card. You could win in a showdown if your weak hand is a little better. If a bet is made, then lay down your hand.

- **Don't be afraid to fold** a fair hand, or even a good one, if you strongly feel that you're beaten. This takes discipline, a very valuable asset to the poker player. Many players just can't dump a pair or better, even if they know they're beaten. Watch for these players.

- **Prepare before the game.** Take a shower and put on fresh clothes. Dress comfortably but not sloppy. This may sound trivial, but if you're clean and comfortable, you'll be more relaxed and alert at the table.

- **Don't drink too much.** Alcohol impairs your judgment and reduces your discipline. It also makes you courageous, generally at times when you shouldn't be. Serious poker players drink very little alcohol, if any. Keep an eye out for drinking players; they'll become reckless and fearless, not easily bluffed.

- **Watch short-stacked (losing) players.** They may try to buy a pot to change their luck. If you hold a fair hand, you should probably call them. Sometimes losing players will get desperate—not a good bluff choice. They may call to try to catch up. If you're losing, don't be desperate; be patient. Bide your time and wait for better cards. By the way, patience is as important as skill and knowledge. Knowledge can be learned, skill comes with experience, but a patient player is a gifted one.
- **I cannot say enough about patience.** I used to drive race cars. After I started playing poker, I found there was quite a similarity between the two activities. No professional in either field can succeed without patience. A race driver will sit driving for hours, watching the traffic, jockeying for position, maybe moving up or down on the apron, calculating movements, drafting behind another car. When the right moment and situation arrive, he guns it, passes, dips, and slips through the other cars.

    The poker player will sit for hours watching the cards and players, waiting, pushing, or laying down. When the right cards and situation arrive, he or she bets all out, raises, reraises, bets the limit, or goes all in. Need I say more about patience?

- **Do not overlook the female player.** Some men don't like playing against women. Remember, she's probably as savvy a player as you'll ever meet; otherwise she wouldn't be there. Respect her at all times.
- **Money management is very important.** If you decide to play regularly, set up a poker bank—money used for nothing but playing poker. This will keep your household finances out of jeopardy. If you're playing in a private game, try to bet conservatively, though not so tight that it's obvious.

    Add winnings to your bank. Never touch the bank for any other reason unless it's large enough that you can treat yourself with the extra.

    If you play in a low-limit casino game, try to leave the game a winner, even if you've played only a short time. There will always be longer playing sessions. Never quit a winning streak; let it quit you. Know when it's over. Set a limit for losses, never for winnings.

- **Keep track of your money or chips.** Know how much you have at all times. Also, monitor your opponents' chips—know who's winning as well as who's losing.

- **Slow down and play fewer hands** if you're losing in a private game. If you continue to lose, apologize, excuse yourself, and leave; no one will blame you. Don't keep playing when you're losing. There's always another night.

  An important point here: It's never a good idea to leave a home game early if you're winning. Your friends may resent your not giving them the opportunity to win their money back.

- **If you're losing in a casino game, it's probably time to leave.** Leaving is no problem to the other casino players; whether you're leaving a winner or a loser, they know someone else will take your seat soon, probably before the next round is dealt.

- **Don't become a show-and-tell player.** Whatever you do in a game, know your good habits as well as your bad. If you can't overcome them, mix them up with your game play to your advantage—try to keep your rivals guessing.

- **Play your big hands hard to drop players after you** if you're in the early or front position—the first, second, or third seat after the dealer (button). The front position isn't ideal, of course, because you're first person to act, and you remain first throughout the hand. The best position is last (button). You get to watch the action before it gets to you. You're the last one to bet, raise, reraise, call, or fold.

- **Poker isn't just about cards; it's about people.** As you sit in games, you shouldn't merely be playing cards; you should be playing the players, analyzing your opponents. Poker is a psychological study of human nature—a glimpse of people at their best or worst. You will see folks act in ways they wouldn't even consider in other social settings. That's why it is important to be an honorable, respectable player—people are watching you. Be a good loser as well as a good winner.

- **Remember that cards run.** Poker cards have good and bad streaks. Learn to recognize when the spell hits and act accordingly. If you're in a losing streak, slow down, play fewer hands, exercise patience, and wait for the cards to turn around. If the bout continues, then you probably should quit for a while. There are no odds or law of averages to tell you when a session will end. If you hit a winning streak, ride it for all it's worth. Keep pushing the bet and being aggressive.

- **Never play too many hands.** This is probably the biggest mistake that novice or inexperienced players make. It refers to playing almost anything you get to make a hand or just stay in the action. Watch for this behavior in your opponents, too, because these players are hard to bluff. Sometimes they get lucky by hitting several winning hands, but most often they're losing players—don't become one of them.

- **Take care of yourself.** Before long-playing sessions, lie down, relax, and even take a nap. An exercise program is important to keep blood circulating steadily to your brain for a clear mind. You'll most likely be sitting for hours at poker games. Be sure to get enough nourishment to stay alert and healthy. These suggestions will make you a fit player.

Home or Private Hold 'Em

If you currently attend a regular home or private game, Hold 'Em is probably being played. If not, introduce it—it's very exciting. A home game is relaxing, and you will likely be playing with friends or acquaintances. The limits usually fit nicely into your budget, allowing you to play more hands and enjoy the game.

Back in the 1970s, when I started playing home games, several of my friends had never heard of Hold 'Em. Once I introduced it, it became one of the most popular of our games. In our group, we rotated homes, with the host providing the refreshments.

Turn back to the Best Starting Hands Guide earlier in this book, and study it carefully. Whenever you can see the flop for little or nothing, do so. The flop will determine whether you should fold or continue. The same holds true with 4th and 5th Street—in low-limit games, the cost will be minimal, and you'll have a chance at making more of your hands. I don't recommend that you see the flop every time if it's going to cost you too much.

Serving as the dealer has two advantages for you. First, you get to observe the actions of the other players before the bet gets to you. Second, you're the last to act throughout the entire hand, giving you the opportunity to see how the others are betting. If your hand is weak and there's no betting, you can raise to drop players. If your hand is strong, you can raise the bettor. Being last gives you some control of the game from the start.

You'll find looser players in low-limit games. Usually, the higher the limit, the better the players.

Play aggressive. Seldom bluff. It's hard to bluff someone for a $1 bet or even a $2 limit—you'll nearly always get a call.

Always act professional. Be courteous to the host and players, especially if it's your first visit—remember, you're a guest, and you might want to be invited back.

If you host a game, set comfortable limits. You don't want anyone losing an embarrassing amount that could cause hard feelings among friends.

Don't gloat or brag about your winnings. No player likes defeat thrown in his or her face. You'll get enough heckling from losing players. If you have weak or inexperienced players in your game, don't berate their poor play—you don't want to run anyone off. Rather, lay it off to "bad luck." Be a good winner as well as a good loser.

Casino Hold 'Em

The casino is a whole other world. You'll be almost intoxicated by the excitement of a poker room with its numerous live games in progress, players moving in and out, cocktails being served, the scents of felt and leather, and the clinking of thousands of chips.

After gaining experience in private games, you might indeed want to try your luck in a casino. What are the differences in the game itself? In the casino, the dealer is permanent, and only chips are used. Antes are rarely used in casino games; they've been replaced by the blind bets known as the big blind and the small blind. Sorry, no more matchsticks or toothpicks.

Somewhere near the entrance you'll find a Limits and Rules Board. This board will show you what type of games are being played, along with their limits, blinds, buy-ins, and rules. Some poker rooms include a seating chart. For beginners, of course, all of this may just as well be written in Greek. Take heart; once you learn the code, everything will become clear. For now, just tell the card room manager that you're new, and he or she will gladly give you guidance. Staff are very helpful. Don't forget that policies vary from casino to casino.

If you feel uncomfortable at first, watch the proceedings for a while. There are nine to ten players at each table. When you're ready to join in, start at the lowest limit. High-stakes and no-limit games can be very intimidating.

After you're given a seat, I suggest that you not play the first couple of hands—don't even look at your pocket cards. Even some pros do this when they start at a new game. Watch the action and get familiar with the procedure of the game, the dealer, and players. You'll feel more at ease after a few moments. Casino play is faster, steadier, and more highly structured than your home game.

There are some differences between home and casino strategy that you should keep in mind. First off, play tighter. That is, play only your best starting hands (as shown in the guide earlier in this book). Be tough before the flop by raising and reraising when you're holding strong cards. If your hand improves after the flop and there are callers, keep the pressure on. Don't make it easy for them to see another card.

If you're on one of the two blinds, it means that you're putting up chips for everyone else to play, so they're seeing their first two pocket cards for nothing. You, on the other hand, have "paid" to see your two cards. No matter what cards you get, see the flop—you're already "in" that game. Other players will have to bet or fold. So if you're *not* on the blinds, you see your first two cards free.

Save your money for the big hands. The come-in bets will add up quickly if you stay for every flop. Only amateurs play every hand. Also, try a bluff when the opportunity presents itself.

When you win a pot, it's customary to tip the dealer. In a low-limit game, generally this means a $1 chip for an average pot; $2 or up if it's a sizable win. Remember, tips come out of your playing bank, and they'll add up if you have a long session. Note that the dealer also draws chips from the pot; this is the house percentage take.

Some card rooms now have automatic shuf-flers built into each table that shuffle and rotate the deck of cards after each deal. The dealer gathers cards from the last hand, stacks them in the auto-shuffler, retrieves another already-shuffled deck, and presses a button; the shuffler disappears into the table, along with the used deck. You're getting a different deck with each round of play.

Many poker rooms feature a kill game. Should a player win two hands in a row, the blind and limit automatically double. A 3/6 game thus becomes a 6/12 game. The kill stays in effect until that same player loses, at which time the game returns to its original limits. Stay out of the kill game until you're more experienced and confident in the procedures of the game.

Should you hit a losing spell, there are a number of things you can do to combat it. Relax and have a drink—but not too much. You'll note that most poker players drink bottled water, coffee, orange juice, and soft drinks. Also:

- Ask for a new deck of cards.
- Change tables.
- Change seats.
- Take a walk; you can even change the casino.
- Whatever you do, don't just sit there.

The Bluff

The bluff is to poker what the old double reverse is to football. You must use it from time to time to keep your opponents off balance. Like the check-raise, it's a valuable tool.

Hold 'Em offers more opportunity to bluff than any other game, given the cards showing on the board and the number of possibilities that can make a hand. Here are a few guidelines:

• The bluff is most successful against one player. If you're trying to bluff more than one, someone may try to keep you honest.

• Make your bluff bet large enough to discourage any calls intended just to keep *you* honest.

• The bluff works best against a tight player. Watch your opponents carefully.

• Bluff early in the game and let it be known so that you're not typecast as a tight player when in fact you rarely bluff.

• Make the same-sized bet when bluffing as betting a strong hand. Your opponents will be unable to determine your style of play. This will keep them off balance.

- A lot of checking and small betting is a good indication of weak hands. This may be a good time for you to try a bluff.
- Keep an eye on your opponents' chips. Players on a short stack might be harder to bluff because they're desperate for a win. On the other hand, in face of a large bet they might fold to save what chips they have left. It's important to study the players.
- Be sure you have enough chips to sacrifice should you be caught.
- Vary your bluff discards. For instance, should you win the bluff, bury your hand and let opponents guess. Next time, turn your cards up to show you were bluffing. This action will keep them off balance.
- To guard against being bluffed, call a bet in a one-on-one situation if you're holding high cards or a pair, or if you have a reasonable investment already in the pot. Win or lose, this will signal that you're not easily bluffed. It's best to do this earlier in the game when you have chips to call and you can expose the bluffer.
- Don't feel you have to keep every player honest. In the end, it'll only drain your chips.

The Board and Reading Hands

These two topics go hand in hand, for it's the information provided on the board that you can use to read what a player may have in the pocket.

Reading hands (determining what a player might hold) is very difficult and comes with experience. I'm not going to dwell on this subject, because the odds on the many different hands can become mind boggling. Odds and percentages is another level of poker well beyond the fundamentals.

Still, here are some basic guidelines in determining what a player might have by what's showing on the board:

- **A pair** on the board could mean a player is holding three of a kind or two pair.
- **Three of a kind** on the board can mean a full house or even four of a kind.
- If a **two-card flush**—say, Hearts—is flopped, someone may be on a four flush. If three Hearts are flopped, be concerned. Should a fourth Heart come on 4th or 5th Street, it's likely that more than one player has a flush. If

you're on the flush, do you hold the nut, the Ace of Hearts?

- If there's a **three–card straight** on the board, chances are that one or more players will be on that straight. This is why it's important to hold the high cards and eliminate callers before the flop. Frequently, the strength of a hand can be determined by the tempo of raising and reraising. These situations are ideal for a skillful bluffer. It's helpful if you know all the players in your home game or have established tells on opponents at your table in the casino.

Some Thoughts on Sandbagging and the Check-Raise

Sandbagging is a term used in relation to the slow play—betting a strong hand as if it were weak to keep players in. For instance, you check a good hand and call a bet. If you can work the magic to 5th Street, then you can check-raise and reraise.

Generally, there's little you can do to defend yourself against a good sandbagger, for it's difficult to distinguish if a player is on the come or just sandbagging. When a player checks or calls throughout the hand, though, warning lights should go off.

If you hold a decent hand and want to test an opponent, raise before the final bet. If the raise is large enough, he or she will likely fold without a strong hand. A sandbagger will probably call immediately.

If the player calls your raise and then raises on 5th Street, most likely he or she was sandbagging and has the hand that was represented. But is it going to take the pot?

Check-raise strategy is particularly effective along with the sandbagging technique. Most home players don't like it, however, and won't allow it in their games, often believing it somehow unethical. In reality, it's not only a smart move but also an exciting strategy. All casinos play check-raise, so be prepared for it. Real poker players love it. Use it whenever the situation presents itself, and be on the alert for it being used against you. When you have the proper hand to pull it off, it can be just too hard to resist. This is an especially good move when an opponent starts to invest a decent amount into the hand.

To refresh your memory, if you're holding a nut or strong hand and it's your bet, you will first check and wait for another player to bet. When he or she does, you come back with a raise when the bet gets back to you. Thus you're first checking, then raising the bettor in the same round. A ploy designed to get an extra bet into the pot, it's most successful on the final round of betting: Seldom can a player resist betting when the opponent checks. Checking usually represents weakness or uncertainty.

If you use a check-raise too early in a hand, you risk giving the strategy away—or your opponents may also check, thus losing you bets you would have gained on 5th Street. By waiting until the final bet, your opponent will already have invested enough chips in the pot to make the call—he or she will be committed.

On the other hand, an experienced player might perceive the raise for what it is and fold, saving the extra bet.

The check-raise works best against more than one player. Odds are good that one player will call, if for no other reason than simply to keep you honest.

In casino games, when a new player asks, "Is this a check-and-raise game?" the seasoned players will smile and reply, "Yes, but only if you have a good hand." And that is the rule: Check-raise only with a good hand.

An experienced or professional player is quite accomplished using the check-raise technique in bluffing situations. It pays to get to know your adversaries.

Some Thoughts on Tells

Some Hold 'Em players are so readable, it's almost humorous. I played in a private game with a guy who'd puff his cigarette when he was on a good hand. If he wasn't smoking at the moment, he'd light up. What an obvious giveaway!

Another player would give off a huge sigh whenever he bet or raised a strong hand, as if he were relaxed or unconcerned. Seems a person under stress feels a sigh is the best way to appear nonchalant. By the way, the two most prominent tells are acting strong and confident with a poor hand, and acting weak and unsure with a big hand. The third most obvious would be the sigh. I think most players don't even realize they're doing it. Another tell? Looking elsewhere or seeming interested in something outside the table and the game. Still other players become very quiet.

Watch all the players all the time. You want as much information as possible about your rivals. Tells are more prevalent at the low-limit table in casinos or your private game. Rarely will you find tells at the professional or high-stakes level. As a new player, you should of course stay in low-limit games until you're fully at ease with the game.

Study and remember your opponents' habits and behavior patterns. Watch for odd mannerisms; analyze their play. I have heard poker players and writers suggest watching a player's eyes, explaining that the pupils become enlarged or even dilated when someone's holding a good hand. I'm not a medical doctor, so I'm not sure if this is true or not. But I can tell you this: You are sitting too far away to actually see the pupils of anyone's eyes, and the players next to you will be looking elsewhere or at their own cards. So don't waste your time trying to stare someone down. Just play your cards.

Admittedly, folks can become nervous and fidgety when stared at or toyed with. This is why some players wear sunglasses. It's hard to intimidate a piece of dark plastic. But there's another reason why they wear eye covers: They want to observe you without your knowledge. Some aggressive people like to play games and stare you down (just remember: They can't see your pupils).

Of course some players just want to look cool.

Results of the Practice Hands

1st Player: Pair of Queens. Stay for flop.

2nd Player: 5 Spades, 7 Hearts. A weak, low straight. Fold.

3rd Player: 6 Clubs, A Diamonds. With Ace high, stay for flop.

4th Player: 10 Clubs, 6 Diamonds. A weak combination. Fold.

5th Player: 8-J Hearts. Possible flush or straight; stay for flop.

6th Player: 5 Clubs, 3 Diamonds. A weak low straight. Fold.

Flop: Q Diamonds, K Spades, 10 Hearts

1st Player: Three Queens. Stay.

3rd Player: Possible Ace high straight, needs the Jack. Is it worth staying for two cards?

5th Player: Possible King high straight, open on both ends. Stay.

4th Street: 3 Clubs

No help to any players.

5th Street: Ace Spades

1st Player: Three Queens, bets the limit—hoping there's no straight out there.

3rd Player: Two Aces. Might call but should fold. (He decides to fold, feeling his opponent has made the straight.)

5th Player: Has the Ace high straight. She raises and reraises.

Bet is back to 1st Player.

1st Player: He'll probably just call. Now he's quite certain the straight was made, but after going this far, he has to make sure his opponent isn't bluffing.

5th Player: Takes the pot.

How did you do?

Conclusion

Poker, like golf, is a game you'll never max. There are good days where every ball you hit is right on. The next time out it's like you've never played before, and you want to throw your clubs into the lake. No different with poker.

You're just not going to win every time you sit down at the table. You'll have winning sessions, play your cards flawlessly, and praise yourself for being as good as any professional. Then the next time out you'll have a terrible session—bad beats, bad cards, and bad luck—and you'll want to throw the cards across the table (but don't). The best you can hope for is enough consistency to stay ahead or at least even.

A good player will overcome losses. Take it graciously, get over it, and move on. Don't be a whiner, or belittle someone you've lost to. No one likes a bitter loser or a boasting winner. It's just plain ugly and demeaning to fellow players.

Be a player to be respected, win or lose. In turn, respect your opponents.

To become a tough player, you have to be a tough bettor. Whether you're on a strong hand or bluffing, your fellow players will know that the moment you're in the action, it's going to cost them money.

Practice: Repeated exercise of practice hands will prepare you mentally and physically.

Knowledge: Gathering information, specifics, data, and a familiarity with human habits will assist in precise decision making.

Courage: I saw combat in Vietnam and I can tell you, there are times when nothing but pure guts will save you from destruction.

Patience: Wait calmly; persevere. Exercise patience until you're rewarded. It does pay off.

When these qualities are fused, you become a skilled Texas Hold 'Em player. Add a little luck and nobody can keep you from being a winner.

I've tried to give you some of the knowledge you need to be a tough poker player; you must now supply the courage and patience.

And it certainly won't hurt if the elusive Lady Luck smiles down on you.

About the Author

TED PANNELL became interested in poker while serving in Vietnam in 1966–67. After his discharge, he settled in Los Angeles, where his interest in poker increased. He started playing in private games then advanced to the card parlors of Gardena, one of the few places in California with legalized poker.

Moving to Las Vegas in the late 1960s, he worked as a security guard at a hotel-casino and played poker in his off hours, finally doing so full time. Hold 'Em wasn't popular; very few casinos even had poker rooms. Seven Stud and Five Card games were the attractions of the time.

After working as a traveling poker player across the United States, Ted finally settled in Hawaii in 1970. There were no casinos or poker rooms, but he found plenty of private card games in homes and hotel suites. He eventually returned to Los Angeles, where he won the biggest gamble of his life: He met and married his Queen of Hearts. His wife, recognizing his interests in books and writing, encouraged him to attend college, where he majored in journalism and literature.

Afterward, he and his family moved to Gardnerville, Nevada, near Lake Tahoe. Between playing live poker and tournaments, he wrote for a local newspaper as a columnist and string reporter. Ted wrote feature stories on major gin rummy and poker tournaments held at Lake Tahoe and Reno that included the Super Bowl of Poker. In 1994 he authored a poker short story that appeared in *Card Player* magazine.

Ted and his wife now live in Palm Desert, California, near many casinos with poker rooms that feature his favorite game: Texas Hold 'Em.

"You have to bet 'em when you get 'em."